3 projects

designed & published in liverpool UK by shedkm ltd sep 2008 - printed in barcelona by vivapress sep 2008

fort dunlop chimneypot park matchworks II

comment by phil griffin - architectural journalist

this red book completes the 3 colour set of shedkm mini monograph's and celebrates the studio's successful programme of projects completed since 1997. the 3 projects chosen - fort dunlop, chimneypot park, the matchworks II - are all for the same client, but show how shedkm, within it's own design parameters, tackles projects of differing scales and purpose. each one has had a colourful history, a long run-in, but a successful outcome. the first - **fort dunlop** - is also the largest and probably the most well known, sitting directly alongside the M6 as it skirts the city of birmingham. for many years, the semi-derelict dunlop tyre factory stood sentinel on this site - an icon to a lost manufacturing era, and a massive statement in a landscape of change. now completely regenerated, it towers above it's neighbours showing its face as an 11 storey 'blue wall' punctuated by a matrix of portholes and the strong impact of an illuminated sky sign proudly announcing its presence. our next project - **chimneypot park** - is of a completely different genre, yet no less effective in terms of its significance. an estate of 'coronation streets' in salford, was the testbed for re-generation of a completely different kind... a housing experiment to bring back life into an area which in effect had disintegrated due to lack of care, resulting in deterioration of the fabric of 19th century worker's terraces with all of the problems that then accrue. shedkm's approach was to reverse this trend, but without destroying an original pattern which sets the backdrop for the perennial TV series. so chimneypot park's face is the original cottages, cleaned and made whole, but concealing behind (where alleyways once stood), magic gardens and unobtrusive covered parking. the third project the **matchworks II** at speke garston liverpool, is on one hand merely another stage in the re-development of the old bryant & may match factory, yet like the other two, shows in the 'matchbox' a strong and confident 'face' to the outside world - an uncompromising all glass pavilion set on a diagonal axis... further into the site the '1948' building completes the project, with an original style skin over a thoroughly modern interior.

fort dunlop

'fort dunlop is the re-invention of an iconic yet derelict storage warehouse into 300,000 sq ft of quality office space, 100 bedroom hotel, retail and supportive landscape facilities. both the building's transformation in use, and the regenerative perception of birmingham to those travelling along the M6, has been achieved by a simple series of bold architectural insertions which enhance the existing structure whilst breathing a new life into the scheme by using clear considered, expressive design...'

hazel rounding - shedkm fort project director

location

the dunlop tyre factory had been empty for 20 years when english partnership's approached urban splash (then emerging as a new force in regenerating derelict industrial buildings for modern use) to investigate the possibility of an urban renewal scheme. at the time, no viable solution had been found due to the extremely deep plan (52m) and the lack of natural light. in late 1998 shedkm were approached, more as an 'ideas' thinktank, rather than, at that time, project architects. a number of ideas were explored, ranging from a 'drive up' motel, through to residential apartments, light industrial units, studios, startup business offices etc. the problem was immense... without an atrium, the notion of division of space into small packages was impossible. but inserting an atrium was difficult structurally, and wasteful of existing fabric. eventually a mixed use format was proposed, with 3 stories of retail - but the planning application for this became deferred (relying on a central government decision) so was eventually withdrawn. then, in spring 2002, based on the success of shedkm's design for regeneration of the old bryant & may matchworks in speke garston liverpool, the clients asked us to have a fresh look based on a brief for workspace allied with 'minimum demolition'. by this time, english partnership's responsibility for grants had devolved nationally, and in the case of the fort, reverted to the new agency 'advantage west midlands'. in the meantime fort dunlop lay empty but not unused, for its natural position alongside the M6 made an ideal site for advertising which then resulted in the biggest and most visible hoarding in the UK which, not only gave promise of things to come, but also publicised england's world cup dreams - amongst many other things. it's hard to believe that such a large piece of real estate should cause so many problems in finding a viable development solution - teams from both the developers and shedkm visited the lingotto in turin, and other schemes - but the fort, a massive symbol of a past age, remained obdurate, waiting for inspiration.

strategy

preservation of all sound, viable and visually acceptable elements with clear insertions expressive of a new order

retention of 3 main facades - all columns and soffits remain exposed, all of these elements should be conserved in situ

all services, circulation, lifts, stairs and toilets, should be placed in a central spine away from the precious daylight

a new glass facade should form a 'box' behind the existing allowing services space and viable exit & escape distances

resultant 'flexible' floor plans to allow office sub-divisions providing usable areas between 1000 & 53,000 sq ft

a new 'green' roof and viewing promenade should be provided to replace the dilapidated structure and shell

the central spine to be extended into an 11 storey structure, adding area subsequently to be used as a travelodge hotel

new highly visible illuminated roof signage to announce the building's presence to the dense daily motorway traffic

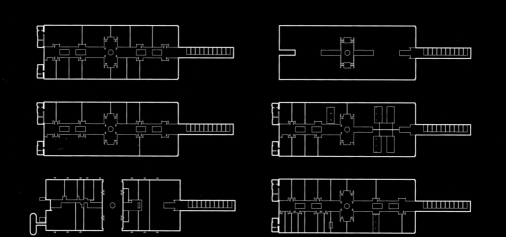

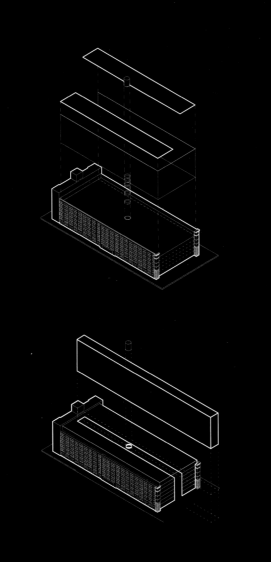

planning consent for 345,000 sq ft (mixed use) was given in 2002. following this, hotel occupier interest was pursued to give 24 hour use to the site. the problem designing in bedroom accommodation, was that the deep plan form made outside awareness virtually impossible to achieve. the solution resolved by shedkm was to extend the core (spine) area outward in a narrow strip 11 stories high. consent for this additional element was given in dec 2003, and a 100 bedroom 'travelodge' hotel was incorporated, marrying up with the 7 stories overall of fort dunlop itself. this became the famous 'blue wall' which has an outstanding visual presence when viewed from the M6 motorway at 70mph!

elsewhere, the idea of a 'box within a box' was used to develop the commercial floors as large open plan offices linked to the central spine which contained all of the service accommodation necessary for toilets, stores, escape staircases and M & E equipment. one of the most difficult elements to resolve in design terms, was the central core with its banks of lifts and escape stairs. at the time, building occupancy was unknown, and a whole series of alternative configurations were researched. the 'as built' solution was for 11 central core lifts and 4 escape stairs giving an idea of the size of fort dunlop which, if viewed through the 4.5m steel atrium drums, is readily apparent.

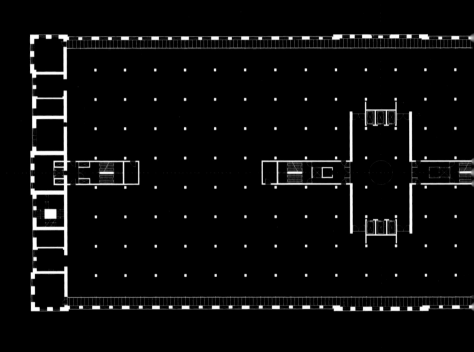

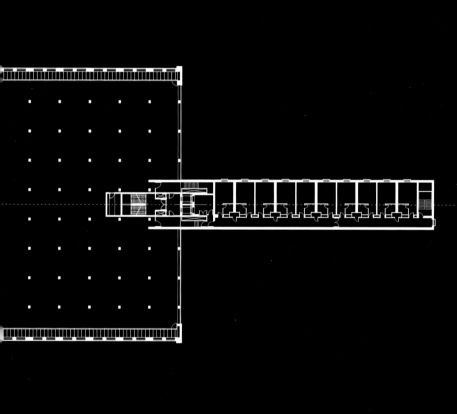

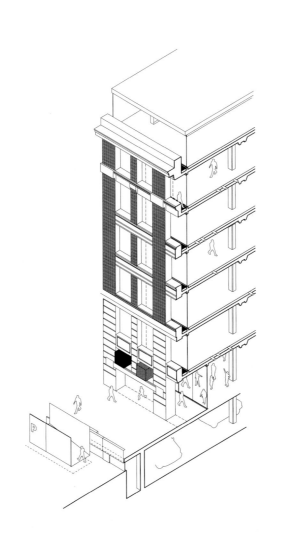

timescale

1998	shedkm approached for participation in ideas forum
2002	planning consent 345000 sq'mixed-use development
2003	planning consent for additional hotel (the blue wall)
2004	first enabling work starts on site - urban splash build
2006	the new travelodge hotel is now open for customers
2006	the main fort building officially opened for business
2007	the building is 97% let (2 years ahead of schedule)
2008	floor by floor fit-out now 97% complete & occupied

construction

the contract, with an original budget of £26M was to be tendered traditionally and a preferred contractor was chosen as a result (taylor woodrow), but in the event urban splash made the decision to use their own in house BUILD. although the fort was somewhat larger than had been previously experienced, the demolition/enabling works programme gave a lead in period which allowed time for a permanent team to be established on site. the newly formed urban splash west midlands subsidiary company set up offices in the fort - shedkm decided to run the job from the liverpool studio, but spending a minimum of 3 days pw on the birmingham site. this arrangement lasted throughout.

the existing building - the old tyre factory - presented complex problems for both contractor and consultants. the frame, although robust in many ways, suffered from extreme dereliction in some parts. and as can be the case in re-generation of old buildings, calculation of loadbearing capacity was a problem with the structural engineers facing much early on site work.   the insertion of the hotel 'spine' with its totally different floor to floor dimension complicated matters, as did the replacement of the existing northlight 6th floor with a new wide span deep build. the north elevation, designed in glass curtain walling, and the roof promenade 'pier' with green roof below, completed the main elements.

'although a high standard of build quality at fort dunlop has been delivered, maintaining this quality throughout the programme can be described as a difficult task. this is due to the phased occupation strategy which was implemented. this was necessary because with a building so large and competing speculatively in an unknown market, it was a risky project for any business to take on. urban splash could not have predicted the speed at which lettings happened so had to use a safer construction strategy in order to keep cost down and ease cashflow...'

PR for the british council of offices award 2008

'retention of the original fort dunlop profile'

'utterly simple detailing and construction'

'visually pure - stripped and calm aesthetic'

'boldly expressive of mass and colour'

'limited palette - steel/glass/render/stone'

'large scale graphics and ancillary items'

'landscape echoes design in scale & colour'

hazel rounding shedkm 2005

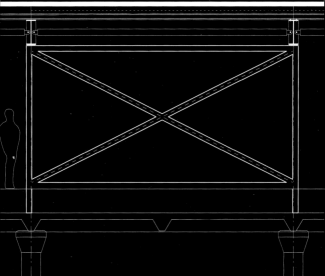

landscape

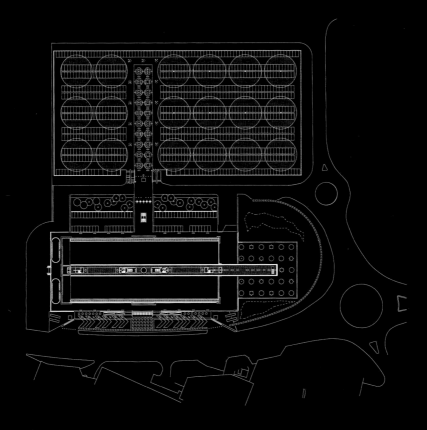

'with a site nearly 3 times as big as fort dunlop itself, our clients have been faced with opportunities ranging from carparking to a massive new office/leisure complex... initially, internationally renowned landscape architects were engaged, but ultimately the task fell to our studio to prepare and implement a landscape strategy. from the rooftop pier like promenade deck across a green roof to the carpark 'roundings' visible from the air, shedkm's ideas were taken on board, developed and eventually commissioned. in the fort, everything you see is upscale - seats, balustrades, walkways & graphics confidently shout their presence...'

from shedkm 'inclusive design' - fort manifesto

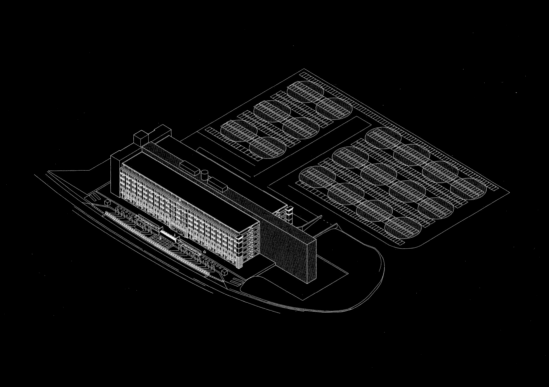

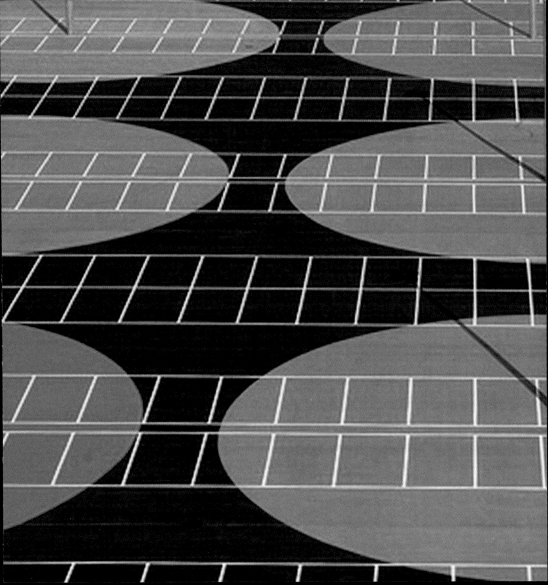

the integration of landscape, graphics and architecture was central to fort dunlop's design integration. from the start the studio proposed that control was exercised right across the development. the identity of the fort was therefore established in a controlled and consistent manner. the idea was that fort dunlop should become a 'brand' which could establish itself as a national identity. this started with the colour orange, the blue of the hotel, black & white and, of course, the re-furbished brickwork and stone of the old tyre factory. a dedicated website was published, with the fort then acquiring attention visually as well as commercially. in marketing the concept, the developer (with input from shedkm) encouraged re-locating businesses to join in with the principles of the architectural transformation and re-brand themselves - becoming part of this new community announcing its presence in the heart of the west midlands. the initiative has proved to be very successful, with businesses from the travelodge hotel through graphic design studios, restaurants, offices and media groups all re-locating. a bus service to the centre of birmingham was inaugurated in 2007, and the inclusion of sandwich bars, a children's play centre and creche, have all helped to support staff out of office activities bringing life to this once derelict and forlorn city fringe. so the 'fort' is more than just a design and construction exercise - it's been something of a com-mercial experiment (risky no doubt), but the success has, we believe, justified the immense time & effort expended on the project. driving north along the M6 is probably the best way to introduce the fort (particularly at twilight). there is no doubting its presence. a massive form with an 11 storey blue wall surmounted by the skysign, is hard to miss. the resemblance to a cruise liner is uncanny - lights blazing, rising in scale out of an inner city fringe of light industrial units, a shopping park, and a waste disposal centre - fort dunlop exudes bravura. there is a fine line between what is brash, and what the critics call 'high architecture' - the fort spans it confidently, portraying an element of both against the night sky.

reality

design & quality control over 350,000 sq' on 7 existing floor plates would be a difficult task in any event for architect and contractor. in the fort, a very pure and symmetrical cruciform plan with longitudinal spine and a central circulation core pierced with 4.5m diameter atrium voids, lays down an order which is hard to break. nevertheless, staged occupancy with a variety of companies each with specific requirements demanded a strong aesthetic as well. so each floor, although tackled consecutively, needed to be able to promote the same strong imagery of detail and graphic design. this is a building of vast apparent space - ideal maybe for city trading floors or call centres, but difficult to partition successfully for the smaller operation. in dealing with this, shedkm provided a dedicated team purely to 'enable' the developer to utilise staged occupancy (businesses up and running whilst build operations continued elsewhere). in fairness, although this involved the architect in an unusual degree of project management, the very success of the venture depended on securing lettings thereby maintaining the lifeblood of cashflow. the idea of 'discerning conservation', whereby building users bought into the concept as well as occupying rented space, seemed novel at first - but with the project's success story now well known it can be said that designing, although a long and demanding process, has been not only an exciting task, but also satisfying - in that phased occupancy has led the architects into close dialogue with urban splash tenants, eventual users of the 'fort'. therefore the architects have always been involved in a continuous process of 'trying to keep the aesthetic and planning ethos of the building, whilst responding sometimes on an almost minute by minute basis to the enquiries and requirements of prospective and existing tenants.' this has been a daunting task over several years... the fort is a very large building indeed - just walking the floors, climbing the stairs takes time. even now the snagging process continues, and with the building almost completely occupied, shedkm are in touch with a whole community of tenants on a weekly visit and daily correspondence basis. the story goes on - there may be more to tell...

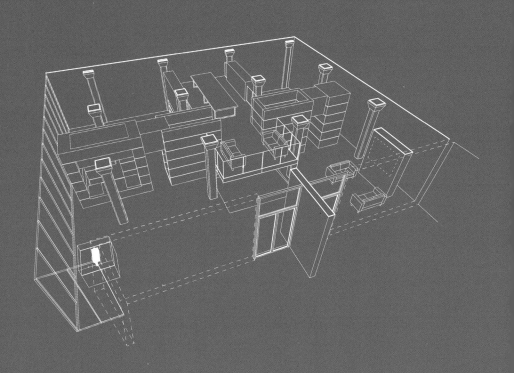

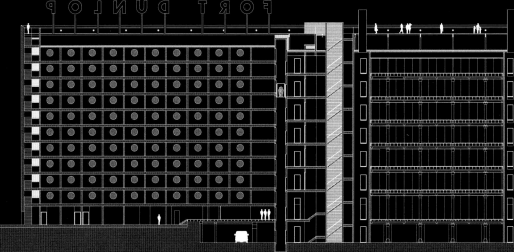

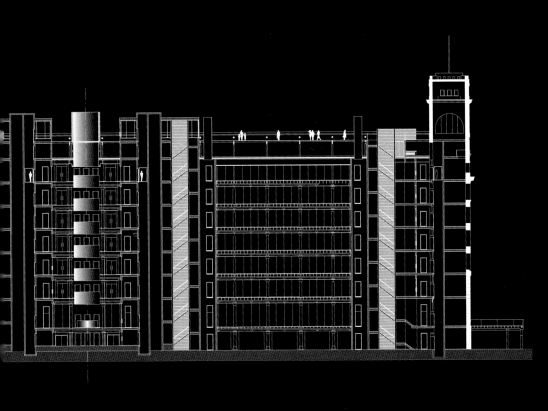

'populated in a clear, financially viable, sustainable and inspiring way, fort dunlop is loyal to its past, present and future use...'

shedkm conservation awards submission - 2007

achievement

'new landmark in a post industrial scene'

'symbol of a resurgent west midlands city'

'great place to work, enjoy and appreciate'

'programme with hundreds of new jobs'

'built statement of confidence and pleasure'

'beautiful image at the motorway epicentre'

'decade of work for architect & developer'

media quotations - 2007/2008

transition

'...for years, fort dunlop was just a large derelict building alongside the M6 at birmingham - of interest more for the words dunlop & 'fort', than for its appearance... now it is a landmark, not only aesthetically, but also as a beacon of post industrial regeneration (big style). so from dereliction to rejuvenation the story of fort dunlop has now passed yet another phase, with hundreds of jobs and dozens of businesses large and small accommodated in this once defunct factory... so what of the future? well the fort has brought people and prosperity to the fringes of birmingham and yet occupies only a fraction of the land available for development. shedkm and their clients are therefore moving to continue the story with a whole series of alternative ideas and concepts. so which one will take hold...? difficult to tell, but such opportunities will certainly not be lost. fort dunlop deserves more, and when things settle down operationally and socially - surely it's ambitions will be fulfiled. in the meantime, tribute is paid to all of those who have made this project happen. it's been a long road over almost a decade, and the result is here to see - so thanks to all concerned - developers, designers, consultants, suppliers, contractors, photographers, writers, agents and of course tenants, users, funding bodies and local authority representatives - all of of whom have contributed to the realisation of the 'fort dunlop' regeneration concept...'

dave king shedkm - september 2008

c

fort dunlop birmingham

site area - 48,625 m2 (4.8625 hectares)

build area - 58,000 m2 (gross - all floors)

project inception - november 1998

current design start date - april 2002

start on site - october 2004

completion - september 2007

fit-out & site completion - april 2008

final cost (inc fit-out) £45,000,000

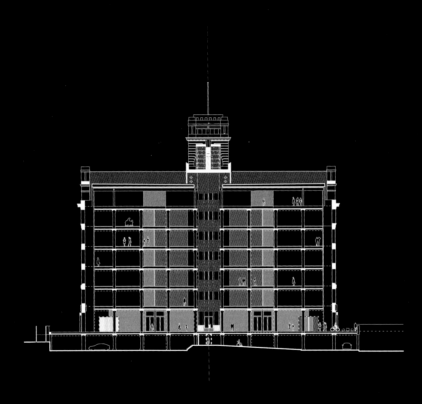

design team

hazel rounding - architect/project director
alan ross - project architect. hotel
mark braund - project architect. basebuild
quentin keohane - project architect. fit-out
steve mccarrick - project architect. fit-out
alex flint - project designer. landscape
+
james weston - architect. development work
neil dawson - architect. development work
ian killick - architect. development work
lee halligan - assistant. development work
bianka schmitt - architect. detail design
ali marshall - assistant. development work
rob jones - assistant. detail design
simon king - assistant. detail design
aparna saligrama - assistant. site inspection
helga steenweg wallin - studio administration

consultants

architects - shedkm liverpool
structural engineers - curtins consulting
QS - simon fenton partnership
M & E engineers - bennett williams
landscape design - shedkm liverpool
signage & graphics - boxer/urban splash
transport engineers - arup transport
planning supervisor - rawlings
building regulations - birmingham city
+
daniel hopkinson - photography
jonathan keenan - photography
ben blackall - photography
morley von sternberg - photography
shedkm - photography + graphics
smoothe 3D - CAD realisations
static & shedkm - models

we would like it to be noted that there are many others in the shedkm studio, and also working for our consultants, who have been involved with and have 'lived through' this project... thanks are due to them, and to all of those from urban splash, BUILD, taylor woodrow, suppliers & subcontractors. also to the photographers who have not been credited individually, but whose efforts are much appreciated in rendering this vast building understandable and hopefully enjoyable in all of its moods, and substance...

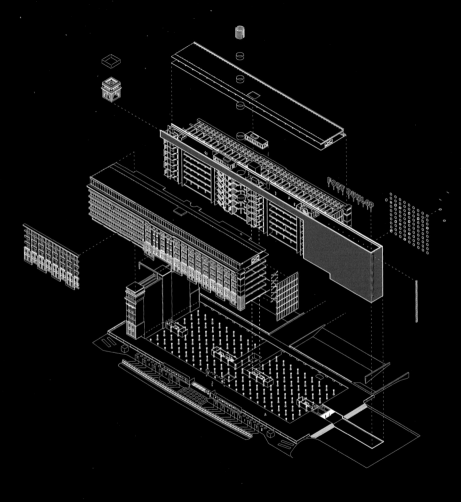

contractors, subcontractors & suppliers

main contractor - urban splash BUILD
mechanical & electrical - mitie
groundworks & concrete - parkstone
groundworks - comanwood
structural steelwork - b & b structures
sundry steelwork - p & s steelwork
structural glazing - solaglass
framed windows - hyatol + baydale
joinery - j + p carpentry
concrete repair & decoration - prestec
stairs - bison precast
masonry - five counties
builders work - jki ltd + holemasters
roofing/waterproofing - james m green
syphonic drainage - rwp
fall protection - total access
rooflight - metclad
circular entrance doors - geze
external doors - accent hanson
internal glazed screens - arkoni
louvres - levolux
passenger lifts - kone
service lifts - independent & saxon

raised flooring - floorplan
finishes - pcs flooring
decoration - APB
bespoke joinery - cw architectural
specialist joinery - SJS
landscape - hortech
supergraphics - gilvar
signage - ASG
furniture - sui generis
access control - secure options
render - astley
+
green roof - bauder
waterproofing - alumasc
render - sto
anti-carbonation - keim
resin floors - remmers
ironmongery - glutz
bespoke sanitaryware - savilles
sanitary ware - armitage shanks
carpets - westbond
landscape units - solway + tarmac
landscape - specimen trees

chimneypot park

location

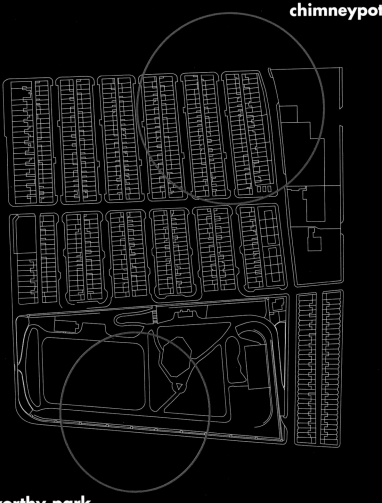

chimneypot

langworthy park

'in 2001 chimneypot park was a rundown group of streets in salford with some properties boarded up and back alleyways overgrown and strewn with litter. the area swung between a no-go ambience and family lifestyle which had been forced to mere survival in a community that had been known since childhood. then - with local authority funding coupled with private investment, 'langworthy' - as it had been called started on a huge transformation which was to have a new name, a new ethos, and was destined to set new standards for the renewal of coronation street style terraces in situ, as opposed to them having to be subject to 1960's style comprehensive redevelopment...'

james weston - shedkm project director

philosophy

shedkm's approach to the problem of how to regenerate langworthy was compounded by on one hand, salford council's desire to provide an element of social (or at the very least 'affordable') housing for first time buyers - and on the other the necessity for it to be a profitable enterprise for a developer.   without a solution that answered both of these objectives, such a project would not be feasible.   in tackling the problem, james weston of shedkm working with nick johnson & nathan cornish of urban splash, moved towards a 'retain the existing street pattern' strategy, which by default soon progressed to retaining the existing terrace houses as well... as a desirable objective, this idea had much to offer - coronation street style with a 21st century twist? - human scale, existing fabric, tradition. in practice this was something of a dream, as modern lifestyle demands modern accommodation, modern living needs space and light, secure car parking, outdoor terraces for outdoor activities, stylish interiors, sophisticated kitchens and bathrooms.   could this really happen in 2 up 2 down victorian worker's terraces - why not clear the whole site - redesign, rebuild?   the solution that emerged after a lengthy design research period was perhaps novel, soon to be christened by the press. the 'upside down houses' (as they became) seemed to attract controversy and some adverse comment - not least from fellow architects. nevertheless the solution, which was to place the daily living accommodation in the top of the house with the bedrooms on the ground floor, proved to be the crucial move that allowed these tiny terraced houses to seemingly expand their spaces, thereby becoming light and airy buildings of their time.   a matrix of quiet terraced streets, trees and nostalgic brick facades with round arch doorways, would reveal modern interiors, precise detailing, stylish staircases and rooms, innovative kitchens and bathrooms and most of all, a magic world of first floor level garden terraces - full of flowers, barbecue decks, safe walkways. and the kitchen in the roof?   more of this later....

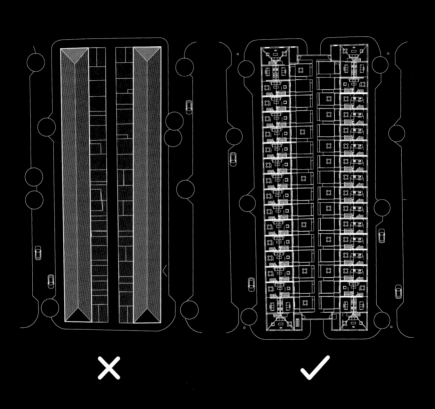

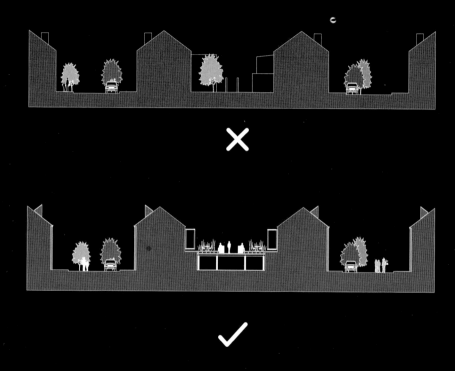

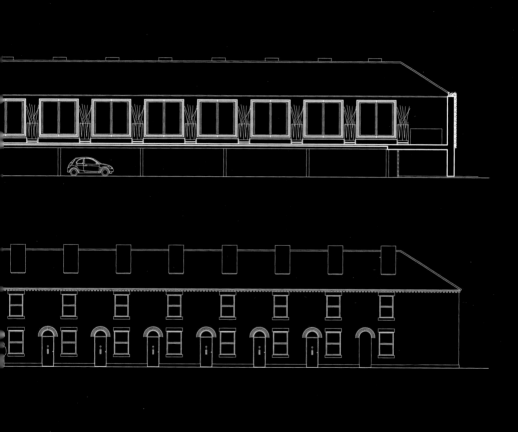

objectives

'modern living in traditional street patterns'

'retention of existing profiles and facades'

'removal of the arbitrary rear extensions'

'provision of secure covered rear parking'

'landscape of communal & private spaces'

'access at lst floor level to garden terraces'

'distinctive character of streets is retained'

architect & client objectives

construction

for langworthy to become 'chimneypot park', a build strategy was evolved which tackled the 10 streets in a cumulative programme which, not only allowed for a learning process to develop for both architect and contractor, but also gave the developer comfort - in that phased marketing and occupation was possible. the process began street by street - initially it was thought that the existing shells of the terraces would be substantial enough to be stripped out internally, then infilled with new structure, services and finishes. in practice however, this proved financially impossible within UK VAT regulations, so a total new build solution was therefore essential. therefore, in order to maintain the traditional langworthy ethos, but provide a new lifestyle opportunity, the decision was made to retain and make good the street facades, then to build the new core structure behind. this practice of facade retention (not uncommon even in listed buildings) threw up subsidiary hurdles ie; what kind of structure - how is the existing supported during enabling works, what are the cost implications etc etc. once decided by the design team (which would include the contractor), the project would (theoretically) be repetitive, easy to programme, and easy to build. this apparently clear road map for construction was however tested to the full, as the reality was that no street was exactly the same dimensionally, each house unit had its own special problems in demolition and facade retention and the rolling programme, although efficient in terms of procurement of materials and subcontract work, would keep shedkm involved at a close level of detail and management over a considerable period of time - even though the contractor (BUILD) took the decision at an early stage to use a steel frame system for speed and expediency. the process of demolition, foundation work, frame erection, infill and finishing can be seen almost as a production line at chimneypot park. as phase 1 finishes and is occupied, so phase 8 begins with site clearance - the illustrations show a snapshot of the process...

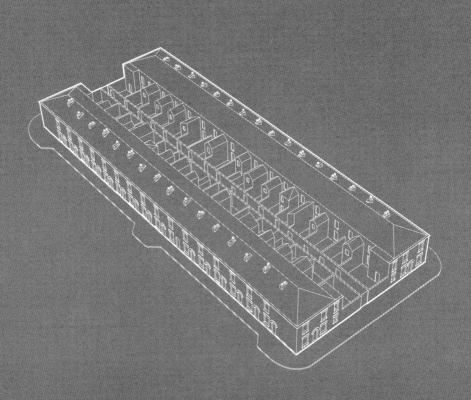

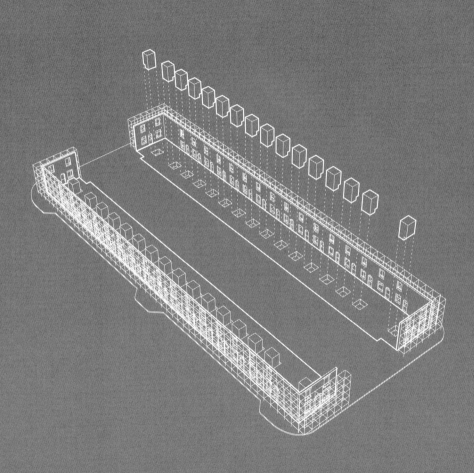

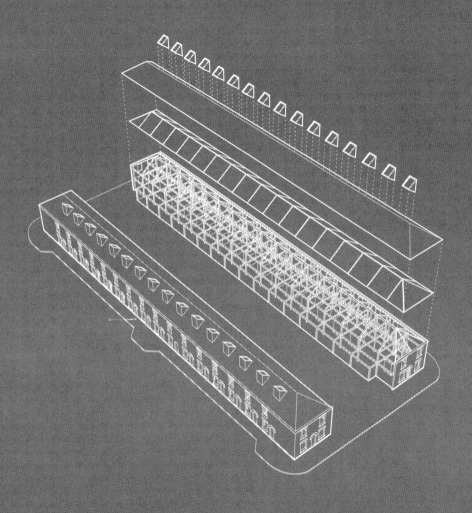

'the building of chimneypot park was something of a learning process all round. at first, we all thought that repetition would make life easy. on the contrary, subtle variations in unit size and layout, when coupled with the exiguences of site dimensions (these streets never quite hit true parallel geometry), tended to make every junction a different problem, and therefore constant attention was the order of the day. completion of phase 1 was something of a milestone as many of the more obvious snags had been highlighted and minor problems solved. nevertheless site visits still continue with half of the total development now handed over. the construction of chimneypot park has become a way of life...'

martyn thomas - project designer 2005/2008

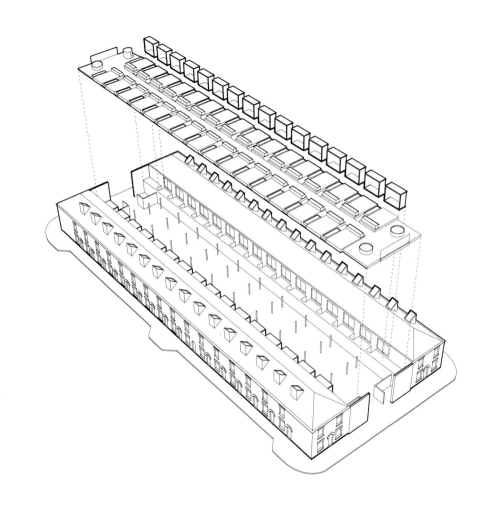

lifestyle

designing for a 21st century lifestyle in streets of victorian workers' terraced cottages was always going to be difficult. for a start, the 2 up 2 down typology was restrictive, the built in amenities were from another age, a sense of light and space did not exist. nevertheless, despite these disadvantages the houses had still been homes, there had still been a strong community - generations had lived and died in this very traditional northern background. the sponsors of the regeneration, salford city council, the manchester methodist housing association, and the northwest development agency (NWDA) were very conscious of this in their brief, and the developers and shedkm strove to retain the area's ambience as a backdrop for a modern lifestyle. in truth, there were still some residents on site (15 or so households) when the scheme eventually was due to begin, and as always is the case, there was some opposition to change. the reality was, however, that most families were happy to move to nearby property modernised under an 'enveloping' scheme thereby allowing old streets the freedom for change. also, a proportion of the newbuild 'chimneypot park' would be made available to first time buyers at very preferential rates. so on the design front probably the first priority would be modern bathrooms and kitchens - traditional post war symbols of social progress in inner city areas such as salford. next would be space and light - suggesting images so often seen in developers' PR material and the sunday supplements, but in fact reflecting the lifestyle that came in the latter part of the 20th century with increasing prosperity and sophisticated taste. therefore the interiors became the first stage in refining the overall concept into a simple buildable format, which although in principle might at first seem just a straightforward 'housebuild' - is in reality light years away from the UK estate builder's norm. the sharp detailing, the GRP bathroom with its sunken bath, the corian kitchen, the sheet glass stair balustrades - all shedkm standard issue, but a breakthrough for langworthy, salford.

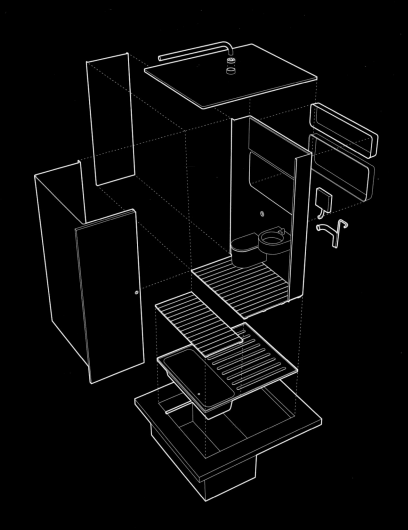

upside down

'...the challenge of re-creating the victorian street pattern in terms of 21st century living rested on the the idea of the 'garden deck'. interiors, yes - modern (as shown), but an accessible garden with private spaces where there was once a dirty alleyway? the solution, which was to place everything at first floor level with parking below was seen by some as too big a risk. nevertheless the developer was up for it and we went ahead. the result speaks for itself - a long planted landscape with a hierarchy of spaces leading from a narrow walkway through steel planters to each individual home's piece of 'indoor/outdoor' defensible space. as can be seen, this was the making of the scheme in a big way...'*

shedkm project team 2005/2008

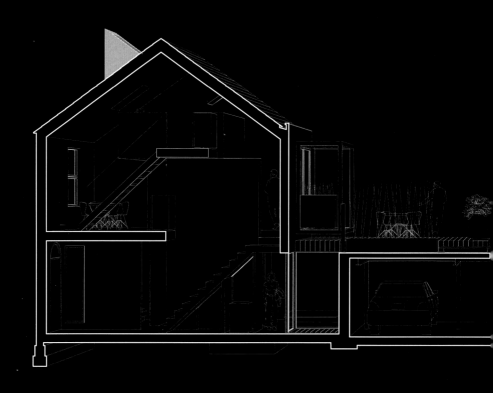

chimneypot park - salford

site area - 2.5 hectares

build area - 10 streets, 418 houses

project inception - autumn 1999

current design start date - march 2000

start on site - february 2006

completion - november 2008

fit-out & site completion - phased

final cost - £26,000,000

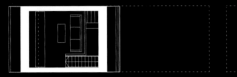

2nd floor

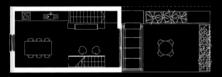
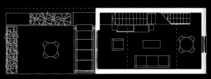

1st floor

ground floor

design team

james weston - shedkm project director
martyn thomas - assistant project director
lee halligan - assistant, architectural design
carrie balmer - assistant, architectural design
david shanks - assistant, architectural design
+
jamie beckford - assistant, architectural design
gareth bansor - assistant, architectural design
tony burke - assistant, architectural design
joerg schulte-wien - assistant design architect

consultants

architects - shedkm liverpool
structural engineers - joule consulting
QS - simon fenton partnership
M & E - inhouse
landscape design - shedkm liverpool
signage & graphics - shedkm liverpool
planning supervisor - rawlings
acoustic consultants - rw gregory
photography - morley von sternberg
jonathan keenan. shedkm

thanks also to all of the others who have been involved in the conception and realisation of chimneypot park - some for a very long time indeed... on site, 10 streets of houses takes patience and resilience, and the core staff of urban splash BUILD have certainly shown this. also others at shedkm and various others including UNIFORM - 3D realisations, and A models. chimneypot park shows the way for future sustainable, affordable housing stock with a modern face in a traditional environment

contractors, subcontractors & suppliers

main contractor - urban splash BUILD
demolitions - windmill demolition
electrical installation - MG electrics
heating & plumbing - RAD
damproofing - specialist remedial
groundworks - williams construction
structural steelwork - harry peers
sundry steelwork - ashton engineering
window repairs - magic man/scratch
framed windows - velfac & maitland
joinery & kitchens - arnold laver
built in furniture - SJS
site works joinery - sunhall
general joinery - oakhill
roofing/waterproofing - mac roofing
grouting & plinths - JV & M donlon
patch brickwork - kevin byrne
replacement cills & arches - LCS
bathroom pods - offsite solutions
gardeners - R E & L thurlow
glass repair - re-new glass
front door fit - S & C developments
scaffolding - UK scaffolding

window protection - swift installations
brickwork - sinclair spatial & ismael
roofing - SIP build
gates & bollards - access & security
street sign & numbers - chris benson signs
spiral stairs - bespoke interior projects
carpets & oak flooring - bogans
brick cleaning - burnaby stone care
plastering & partitions - C & P partitions
metal & planters - central steel
water services - connect utilities
decorators - craig more
staircases - darcy joinery
decking - edward oliver joinery
decking grillage - engineered composites
terrace resin - hi-bond contracts
mirrors - j price (glazing)
clean units - B & M cleaning
door furniture - RBAI
entrance doors - performance doorset
lintels - pre-cast concrete structures
trespa panels - vivalda ltd
security - bonded security

matchworks II

matchbox + the 1948 building

the matchworks story began in 1996 when 4 people - tom bloxham, bill maynard, dave king & jonathan falkingham visited the derelict bryant & may match factory at speke/garston liverpool on a cold windy winter's afternoon. afterwards, in the garston arms hotel, surrounded by pint drinking locals, tom's 'vision' for the matchworks was born... a straight line drawn through the whole ensemble of industrial building and associated detritus challenged the architects to translate that beer-mat diagram into reality. now, 12 years later, another phase has been completed, adding to the multi-award winning commercial development known as the **matchworks**. the 'matchbox', together with what is known as the '1948' building follow closely in both position and presence a first KM development plan, which provided a strategy for incremental development to cover the whole site with a selection of converted spaces following closely the strong geometry set out by the original jan bylander structural grid (thought to represent europe's first example of a US style flat slab construction process). the matchbox itself, a pure square in plan, is set on a diagonal layline which bisects the site, using the old water tower as a fulcrum, and placing the new building in a corner position announcing the whole development to visitors arriving via the nearby john lennon airport. the 1948 building - a conversion/newbuild, lies behind the matchworks with its steel canister shaped service pods, enclosing a large landscaped rear courtyard. two different buildings... yet there is an aesthetic continuum. the **1948** building with its strict planning around yellow internal service pods, is approached by a steel walkway - the matchbox by a formal entrance facing the matchworks itself on the diagonal. the 1948 building is linear on a sloping site - whilst the matchbox, formal in the extreme, sits over a grassy mound inspired by chermayeff's einstein tower at potsdam. the project architects themselves form a continuum too - king mcallister, then the amalgamated shedkm, then ultimately 'snook' founded by neil dawson (project architect at shedkm). the matchbox is shedkm's first greenfield site building for urban splash. future phases are planned - the 'matchstick' being the first so far.

matchbox

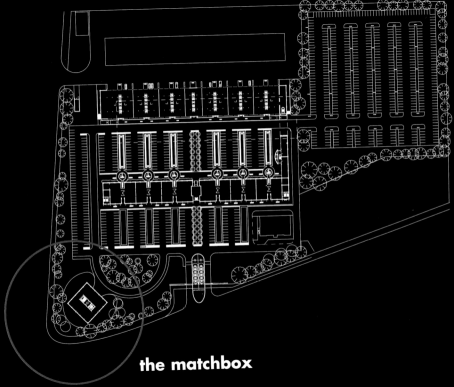

the matchbox

'*...this was always a fantastic site. I remember passing it and thinking - what a group of buildings, so sad to see them empty...   later, when we eventually started to look at the problem in detail, a knife had to be used to cut away so much industrial detritus. in the end phase 1 of the matchworks with its red 'chimneys', black pipe seats and entrance portals, became an icon of the south liverpool approach. only a brave 'in your face' building could better this on the site, and the matchbox does the job with aplomb. it's the first piece of modern architecture surely worthy of an award on the airport road. the night of the table football league - the sun on the silver frame against a dark sky. raw concrete, lime trees - maybe next year they say... we can wait'*

dave king - shedkm

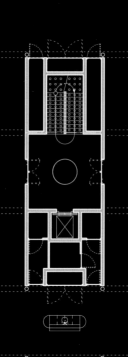

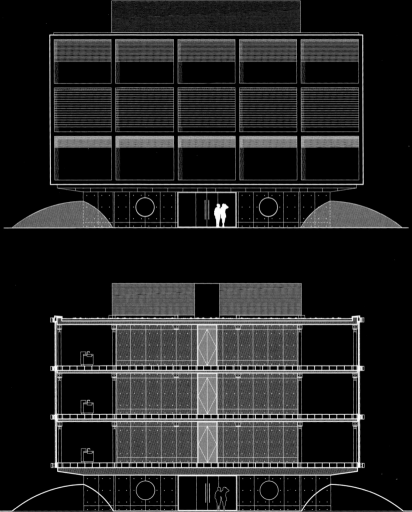

the matchbox - as a concept - is a steel and glass pavilion placed diagonally at the corner of the matchworks site. as a commercial development, it is 3 floors of open plan, flexible, air conditioned space arranged around a central staircase and lift core with a ground floor reception, services and conference room facility. in fact though, the matchworks is more than this... it is an example of an acutely detailed concrete, steel and glass building with reference to architects such as mies and craig ellwood. structurally, a concrete transfer slab cantilevers over the grassy mound and supports a steel perimeter frame spanning back to the in situ concrete core. outside this basic structure with its round columns and capitals, the outer 'window' frame assembly gives the building its distinctive character. this outer frame uses (to some eyes) 'oversize' sections, which stand slightly clear leaving space for external blinds to be incorporated on all four elevations. the blinds themselves add to the almost abstract appearance which can change from solid to void, reflective to transparent at the touch of a button. internally, the central core is formal and ordered with a narrow atrium using shedkm trademark circular steel balustrades surmounted by a 'chimney' rooflight echoing the matchworks detail. bright red teapoints are placed on each floor - the yellow male and female washrooms are unusually narrow and high, and the stair itself is arranged around a raw block wall with pre-cast treads with stainless flat section balustrade. the effect is very simple and straightforward and the plan is particularly easy to read. each floor can, in fact, be subdivided into two or 4 business units with the services (lighting and power) having been laid out to allow this. the ground floor is directly accessed from the main entrance and can again be subdivided into conference/seminar rooms, or left open as exhibition space. the matchbox is clear, simple and has the directness of a classical pavilion with a sweeping semi-circular driveway and a formal entrance. the first function to be held there - the 'match of the day' table football league - was an instant success, and currently the addition of a group of superlambananas looking out through the glazed facades has contributed to liverpool's 2008 celebrations with some style.

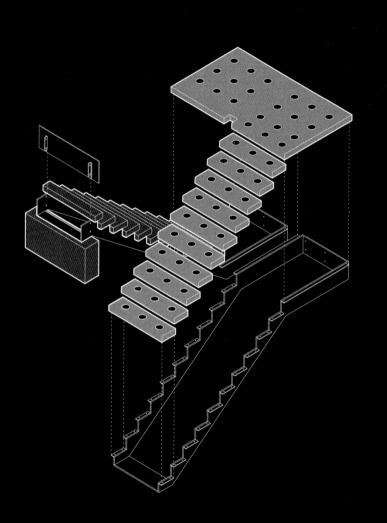

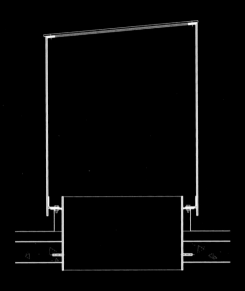

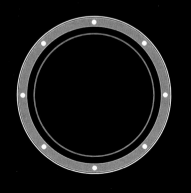

'a building to exhibit exposed finishes'

'in-situ concrete, blockwork, steel, glass'

'using pre-cast beams & exposed services'

'sheet steel balustrades, pre-cast treads'

'stainless steel handrails - all flat section'

'use of 2 primary colours in small amounts'

'silver auto-control sunblinds in every bay'

design criteria for the matchbox

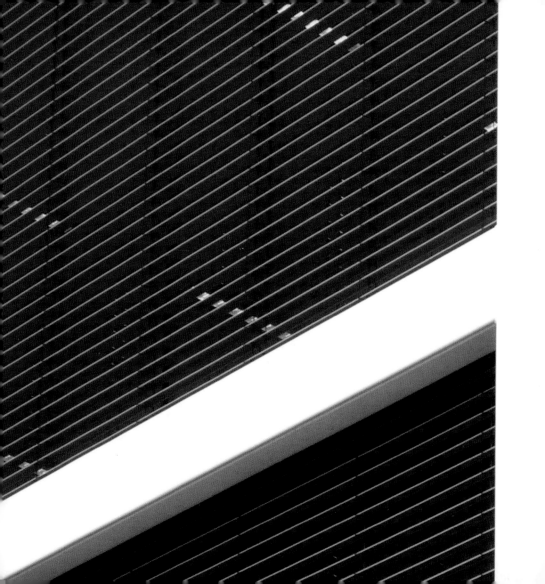

1948 building

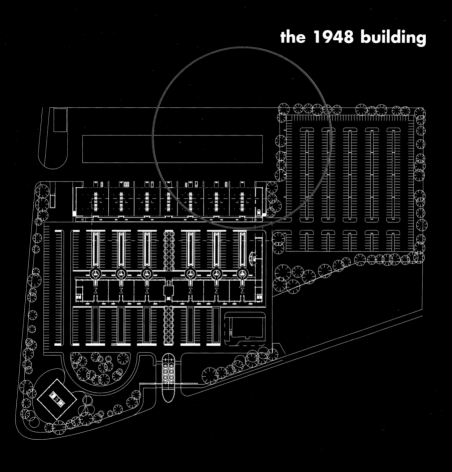

the 1948 building

'when the demolition lads got on site, they virtually removed the building! we had all thought that our original idea for a new build was the most sensible, and it certainly was beginning to look that way. the 1948 building - almost an afterthought - had been on the horizon for a long time. a logical progression as per the masterplan, open space planning etc, and here was just a ruin with only a few columns standing! but as we began to rebuild those walls, bit by bit, we were encouraged by the original proportions and window types. the simple plan with its very clear cores took shape, and a new roof with an elegant twin beam structure echoed the forms in phase 1. the 1948 building remains a very simple concept indeed - satisfying...'

neil dawson - project architect

the 1948 building - bryant and may's original match store with it's giant sprinklers fed from the iconic watertower was, in a sense, always secondary. the lower storey was a close grid of massive columns holding up jan bylander's innovative flat slab, and the upper a lightweight warehouse with brick and glass outer walls aping the grade II listed as found on the matchworks itself. as a scheme in the making, there were many proposed transformations ranging from simple carparking, a call centre for abbey national (as it was then), to a combination of economic business units over light industrial spaces below. designing out the site change in level and getting access to the higher floor whilst retaining some light to the lower, necessitated a long pedestrian deck bounding the matchworks rear courtyard, and a system of shutters at lower level which would allow tenants to use the space as drive in, or as offices. as in the matchworks itself, semi abstract forms abound with entrance portals, tubular seats, flat steel balustrades and of course the yellow cores which divide the upper level into a terrace of 'pavilions' on the same grid as phase I. in the '1948' building contract, the link - known as the west wing and bridge, has been re-established in a differing form with an escape stair concealed in a submarine conning tower like tube and three new round windows over the bridge link itself. the 1948 building has now established itself in its own right, with its own character - similar yet different, familiar but new. an interesting combination and ironically, successful in that a reconstruction in what could be said to be the original style, has produced a completely modern building suitable for 21st century occupancy. in addition to this, a visual link to the original grade II listed matchworks has provided a sense of enclosure with trees and seating - something that was entirely lacking in the original factory. shedkm's masterplan of 1997 foresaw this, as it did other development potential. flying in to john lennon airport, the matchworks site is clearly visible, and the 1948 building with its matching grid shows how much thought the original matchworks architects must have given to the overall terms of the site layout.

transformation

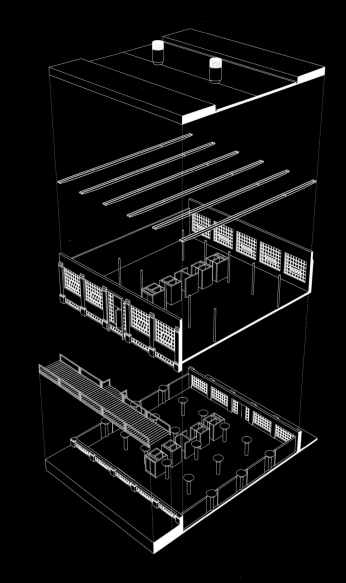

continuum

'new build & regeneration in harmony'

'a continuation of the bryant & may style'

'use of the shedkm colour & detail palette'

'the idea of united terraced pavilions'

'the creation of wide & spacious piazzas'

'use of distinctive red portals at entrances'

'sharp steel details complete the landscape'

matchworks design - 2008

'...satisfying, yes agreed (eventually), but the whole matchworks history has been one of stop start, what next, will it won't it?   to be fair though, liverpool is often like this as yields have been traditionally low, and developers cautious.   nevertheless here we are 11 years into the story and it's still going, still offers chances of new build, conversion, landscape - all on what was industrial dereliction with only ghosts of the past to testify for the once vibrant bryant & may factory with its 'matchgirls', brass bands, oversize sprinkler system and mass employment in south liverpool. it's now the NHS primary care trust, ACAS, & the callcentres which have taken over.   matchworks II with the new build matchbox, the re-juvenated 1948 building, holds promise of a whole new international style airport city but with undertones of it's past...'

dave king - shedkm

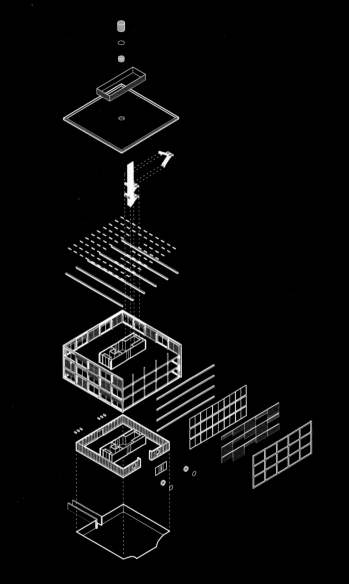

matchworks II - speke/garston

build area matchbox - 4300 m2 gross

build area - 1948 building - 8200 m2 gross

project inception - january 1997

current design start date - autumn 2002

start on site - summer 2005

completion - march 2008

final cost - £8,500,000 (both buildings)

design team

neil dawson - architect/project director
rob jones - assistant. detail design
dave king - architect. concept
miles pearson - assistant. concept
saskia fink - assistant. concept

consultants

architects - shedkm liverpool
structural engineers - bingham davis
QS - simon fenton partnership
M & E engineers - PSD
landscape design - shedkm liverpool
signage & graphics - shedkm liverpool
planning supervisor - rawlings
building regulations - liverpool city

contractors

main contractor - urban splash BUILD
in situ concrete - ADANA.
electrical installations matchbox - MG electrics
electrical installations 1948 - cegelec
water & heating services - townley & hughes
matchbox steelwork - MSR
1948 steelwork - shawton
matchbox glazing OJ taffinder
additional steelwork - ashton engineering
raised floors - quillingotti
1948 windows - clement windows
roofing - alumasc
render - CLAN construction
lifts - kone
+
photography - morley von sternberg
additional imagery - dave king

matchworks II has been a long running project with (until recently) intermittent progress. consequently, many people have been involved from time to time, including the liverpool staff of laing o'rourke who developed an initial production information process. thanks are also given to SISK & KIER NW (initial tenderers). notwithstanding a wealth of tender activity at an early stage, thanks are due to the BUILD site teams for doing a great job with little fuss, and - with their sub-contractors - producing excellent quality of detail and material. on the design side, shedkm's input at detail design and site level has been handled by neil dawson who latterly set up his own practice SNOOK to help complete the project on site.

There is a lot that is determined about the architecture of shedkm. Despite splashes of motley – notably Dulux 23 YY – it is a serious, even devout business. If the team was not both skilled and match-fit, schemes such as Chimneypot Park, Fort Dunlop and Matchbox might flare up in the face of their creators.

You need to be sure of your moves when you up-turn a workers' terrace and rob it of its own back yard. You will need to be marathon tuned to slice through Fort Dunlop, slot in a hotel and top it with a timber running track. Matching the 1948 industrial finesse of Jan Bylander's engineering for Bryant and May is no pale ambition. shedkm has flare, discipline, exactitude and a handful of stylistic ticks.

Nowadays fashion designers, graphic designers, and owners of Corbusier recliners are likely to hold architectural views. So much that architecture has been annexed by design and marketing. Planners, project managers and politicians have a lot to say about what buildings should and shouldn't do, how they might look and perform. Reaching the end of a building boom is sobering. What have we got to show? Truthfully, not all that much.

shedkm makes buildings in its own manner. A clutch of signatures; plate steel, circular cuts, cylindrical balustrades, post-Rietveld, Piet Mondrian, de Stijl with a Liverpool twist. Fort Dunlop is big, Chimneypot Park is clever, Matchbox is accomplished. Post-building boom, they are all amongst a relatively small number of schemes that are propping up architecture as a noble profession. So strong is the identity and character of the work of shedkm that the practice is, to my thinking, dangerously close to being that myth of 21st century virtue, a Brand. When you are this good at making buildings, it is difficult to mess up. Which could become dull. Solution? Less time on the training ground, more time in the bar...

phil griffin - august 2008

shedkm has won over 50 major awards in 11 years

7 RIBA awards for architecture

6 housing design awards

4 civic trust awards

3 roses design awards

2 BCO awards

2 MIPIM awards

chimneypot park - top housing design award in 2008

*" Beautiful also with all the animation that the artist's sensibility
can add to severe and pure functioning elements. "*

le corbusier - 'vers une architecture'